Americans All biographies are inspiring life stories about people of all races, creeds, and nationalities who have uniquely contributed to the American way of life. Highlights from each person's story develop his contributions in his special field — whether they be in the arts, industry, human rights, education, science and medicine, or sports.

Specific abilities, character, and accomplishments are emphasized. Often despite great odds, these famous people have attained success in their fields through the good use of ability, determination, and hard work. These fast-moving stories of real people will show the way to better understanding of the ingredients necessary for personal success.

Ralph Bunche

CHAMPION OF PEACE

by Jean Gay Cornell

illustrated by Victor Mays

GARRARD PUBLISHING COMPANY
CHAMPAIGN, ILLINOIS

For David

Picture credits:

United Nations: pp. 60 (top), 68 (bottom), 83 (both), 90, 91 (all), 96

United Press International: pp. 9, 60 (middle), 68 (top), 78, 79, 87

Wide World Photos: pp. 29, 60 (bottom)

Library of Congress Cataloging in Publication Data

Cornell, Jean Gay.
    Ralph Bunche, champion of peace.

    (Americans all)
    Includes index.
    SUMMARY: A biography of a man internationally
famous for his efforts towards world peace.

    1. Bunche, Ralph Johnson, 1904-1971—Juvenile
literature. [1. Bunche, Ralph Johnson, 1904-1971.
2. United Nations—Biography. 3. Negroes—Biography]
I. Mays, Victor, 1927-   II. Title.
E748.B885C67   341.23'3'0924 [B] [92] 75-20368
ISBN 0-8116-4583-5

Contents

1. A New Home

Ralph stared out the train window at endless miles of flat land. Now and then he saw a farmhouse in the distance. He wondered when the train would reach Albuquerque, New Mexico.

Ralph looked at his grandmother, sitting on the seat beside him. Asleep in her arms was his baby sister, Grace.

"How soon will we be there, Nana?" he asked.

"Shhh! Don't wake the baby," the tiny, gray-haired lady whispered. "About two more hours. And an eleven-year-old boy doesn't have to squirm like that."

"It's hard to sit still for so long," Ralph said softly. "Tell me all about Albuquerque, Nana."

"People say it's pretty. There's a big river—the Rio Grande. And there are mountains not far away. But best of all, it's warm and the air is clear—not dirty like in Detroit. Warm, clean air can help your mama get well. And your daddy, too, when he comes to join us. Your daddy's lung sickness makes him cough so much it scares me sometimes."

Ralph looked over at mama, dozing next to Uncle Charlie. "She looks so tired," he thought. Mama always used to be cheerful and lively. She used to love playing the piano. But she hadn't played the piano in a long time. Ralph missed the sound of her music.

8

Ralph Bunche as a small boy

The doctor said she had rheumatic fever. Many days she could hardly get out of bed. Then Nana would send Ralph out of the house to play, so her daughter could rest quietly.

There weren't many places to play in the crowded part of Detroit where Ralph Johnson Bunche had been born on August 7, 1904. His house was crowded too. Besides Ralph's father, Fred, and mother, Olive, Nana's other sons and daughters

9

also lived there. They were a close-knit, happy family. Ralph's grandmother, Lucy Johnson, had raised her five children alone after her schoolteacher husband had died.

Nana had been born a slave. More than anything else, she wanted a better life for her family. She'd seen to it that all the children had gone to school. "A good education is the only way to get ahead in this world," she always said.

The train arrived in Albuquerque at last. Nana and Uncle Charlie soon found a house to rent.

"The next thing is to find out where Ralph will go to school," Nana announced. She wasted no time in entering him in sixth grade at the Fourth Ward School.

Ralph's teacher was Miss Emma Belle Sweet. Ralph had never known a teacher like her. She was a little woman. But she managed the class of 65 students without ever raising her voice. And somehow she found time to be interested in every boy and girl.

Miss Sweet's favorite subject was geography. Her eyes sparkled as she told the children about strange and wonderful places. They were places she had never seen. Yet she made her students see them as clearly as if they were there.

One day when Ralph came home from school, he sat with mama on the porch. As the sun was setting, they watched the purple shadows grow on the mountains.

Ralph told his mother about Miss Sweet's geography lessons. "Someday I'd like to travel to all those places. And I think I'd like to be a teacher too."

Mama put her arm around his shoulders. She smiled her gentle smile. "I hope you do, son," she said. "Don't ever let anything take away your hope, and faith, and dreams. Your father and I would be very proud if you became a teacher."

"When is papa coming to Albuquerque?" Ralph asked.

"Very soon now," mama answered.

"I wish he'd hurry. I miss him. Maybe he'll get well here." Ralph remembered

the sounds of his father's terrible cough. It left papa weak and gasping for breath.

When his father arrived in Albuquerque, Ralph was shocked to see how ill he looked. Fred Bunche had been a barber in Detroit. But his lung sickness had gotten worse, and it was now impossible for him to work. The health of both Ralph's parents became steadily worse. They died within a few short months of each other in 1917. Ralph tried to think that all that was happening was only a bad dream.

One night Nana called the whole family together. Her other son and daughters— Tom, Nelle, and Ethel—had joined them in their time of trouble.

"I think we should leave Albuquerque," Nana said. "There are too many unhappy memories here."

"Do you think we should go back to Detroit?" Aunt Ethel asked.

"Oh, no," Nana said, shaking her head. "I couldn't stand those cold winters again. Why don't we go to California—maybe Los Angeles? I hear there are good jobs there."

Ralph looked up from the book in his lap, and his eyes brightened. Miss Sweet had told the class about California and how beautiful it was. He held his breath, waiting for the others to speak.

"It sounds like a good idea to me," said Uncle Tom.

Ralph could be quiet no longer. "Oh, yes, let's go!" he burst out.

Nana looked into his pleading eyes. "Then it's settled," she announced. "We'll start packing tomorrow."

14

2. Moving on Again

"Oh, look, Nana!" Ralph said excitedly. "Orange trees—lots of them!" His face was pressed to the train window as they neared Los Angeles. There were brightly colored flowers, too, such as he'd never seen before. Ralph was sure he would like California.

Uncle Tom had gone on ahead of the family to look for a place to live. He had found a house in a neighborhood that was mostly white and had paid the owner two months' rent.

Tom was waiting at the station. He was anxious to show the family their new home. They all crowded into a taxi. Everyone was smiling and talking at once. But when they reached the house owner's office to get their keys, the smiles disappeared.

"You didn't tell me your family was black!" the owner said angrily.

Tom, who was very light-skinned like Ralph, said politely, "You didn't ask me."

"Well, I'm not renting that house to *niggers!*" The man banged his hand on the desk.

"You already *have* rented it to us," Nana said quietly. "And we're going to live there for as long as the rent has been paid. Come on, Tom, let's go." She held her head high as she led the group outside to the waiting taxi.

"A fine welcome to Los Angeles," Ralph

muttered. All the brightness seemed to have gone out of the day.

"Don't you mind, Ralph," Nana said. "People can hurt you only if you *let* them. Be proud of your race. One day I'm sure you'll make your race proud of you."

The family settled into their new home. even without the keys. They had to break the door to get in. The uncles and aunts all managed to find work. Soon they had saved enough money for a small down payment on a little house of their own.

Meanwhile, Nana entered Ralph, now thirteen years old, in the Thirtieth Street Intermediate School. Every night Nana asked, "How was school today?" More often than not, Ralph's answer was a bored, "Oh, all right—I guess."

"But you always liked school," Nana said, a troubled frown on her face. Finally, she announced, "I'll meet you at school tomorrow after classes. We're going to have a talk with the principal." Ralph had no idea what his grandmother had in mind. But he knew better than to argue with her.

Seated in the principal's office the next day, Nana spoke up. "Is Ralph getting the courses he'll need to enter college?" she asked.

The principal raised his eyebrows in surprise. "Why, no," he said. "He's taking courses that will help him get a job."

"Sir," Nana said firmly, "my grandson is going to go to college. And it's your job to see that he's prepared for it." Ralph wondered if there ever would be enough money for college. But Nana's voice was determined. Ralph's courses were changed, and a whole new world of learning opened up for him. School was no longer just "all right," it was exciting.

After school Ralph sold papers, as he had in Detroit. One hot summer day the newspaper company he worked for had a picnic and swimming party for all the newsboys. Ralph and the only other black boy in the group sat together on the bus. They had their swimming trunks and towels in hand.

"Boy, that water is going to feel good!" Ralph said, wiping his hot face with his towel.

"I can't wait," said his friend. But at the gate to the swimming pool, they were both stopped by a guard.

"No Negroes in this pool," the guard said. Ralph stepped back as though he'd been struck. He felt sure the white boys wouldn't mind swimming with him and his friend. But Ralph was too proud to argue with the guard. Besides, he knew it would do no good.

That night he told Nana what had happened. She said, "You remember what I
told you? People can hurt you only if you
let them." Ralph sighed. He should have
known Nana wouldn't let him feel sorry
for himself. Besides, he couldn't stay
unhappy very long in his cheerful, loving
family.

In the fall of 1918, Ralph entered
Jefferson High School. Few other black

students attended this school. But then, few had a determined woman like Nana urging them to get more education. Nana carefully went over Ralph's report cards. His grades had to be good enough so he would be accepted into college. Nana could find no fault with his marks. Ralph was a quick, eager learner.

His favorite subjects were history and political science. He joined the debating team, and he learned to write and give speeches. Opposing teams argued different views on a subject. The team that gave the best reasons for believing as it did won. Ralph always enjoyed the debates.

He liked sports too. He was on the baseball, football, and basketball teams. Every chance Ralph had, he practiced shooting baskets or throwing a ball with his friends.

In the summertime he worked hard at

whatever jobs he could get. Ralph spent one summer as a newspaper messenger boy and another as a servant in a Hollywood home. Sometimes he worked as a carpet layer.

Graduation time came near. Ralph's class was told that the names of those elected to the Los Angeles student honor society would be announced. The list was a long one, and Ralph waited to hear his name called. He knew his grades were the highest in the class. But there was no Ralph Johnson Bunche on the list. Once more he had been hurt because of his color.

"I'm going to quit school, Nana," he said when he got home.

"You are *not* going to quit school!" Nana said, banging her fist on the kitchen table. "You're going to graduate from high school so you can go to college, and

that's *that!*" Ralph looked into his grandmother's face and knew how much his graduation meant to her.

"All right, Nana," he said. "You win."

On graduation day Nelle, Ethel, and Nana were dressed in their best clothes. They sat as near to the stage as possible. When Ralph stepped up to receive his diploma, the principal announced, "We are pleased to name Ralph Johnson Bunche valedictorian. His grades are the highest in the class of 1922." Ralph gave a speech that he had written.

After the ceremony Ralph found his aunts and grandmother. "Here, Nana," he said, holding out his diploma to her. "It really belongs to you."

As she reached up to kiss him, Ralph felt tears in his eyes. He was glad he hadn't disappointed her—this fierce little woman who loved him so much.

3. College Days

Ralph received a scholarship from the University of California at Los Angeles. He could hardly believe his good luck. But Nana wasn't surprised.

"Didn't I always say you were going to college?" she asked, a proud smile lighting her face. "You're going to *be* somebody!"

"What I'd like to be is a teacher of political science," Ralph said. "I want to learn everything I can about how governments work—governments all over the world. I can't wait for classes to begin."

All through the summer of 1922, Ralph worked as a carpet layer. It was hard work, but it paid more than most jobs he could find. He needed the money for his living expenses at college.

When college opened, Ralph decided to try out for the football team. He was only average in height, but he was strong and a determined player. He made the team.

After practice one windy day, Ralph was walking off the football field. He felt a sharp pain in his left ear. It seemed as if a needle had stuck him. Ralph shook his head and hurried to the locker room.

The pain grew worse as he dressed and went home. By the next day it was unbearable, and he knew he'd have to see a doctor. The doctor found a small sliver of grain deep in Ralph's ear. The wind had probably blown it in. Now the ear was badly infected.

"I'm afraid we'll have to operate," the doctor said.

The operation was a complicated one. Following it, a blood clot formed and settled in Ralph's left leg. He lay in the hospital for weeks, worrying about the classes he was missing. He worried, too, because the hearing in his left ear was damaged.

When Ralph was able to leave the hospital, Nana took him home and cared for him. She cooked his favorite foods, for Ralph loved to eat. She brought him stacks of library books. And slowly, he began to get well.

At last, in the fall of 1923, Ralph returned to college. He found a place where he could live free of charge by doing odd jobs for the owner of the building. He earned money for his other expenses by cleaning stores and offices.

Somehow he also found time to play basketball, football, and baseball. During his sophomore year, he decided to limit himself to basketball and work really hard at that. He was soon a star guard on the varsity team.

UCLA and Stanford were both in the Pacific Conference. That year Stanford had a powerful team. Few people thought UCLA had a chance of beating them.

Ralph was a star guard on UCLA'S basketball team.

When the game started, Stanford began piling up points. But Ralph was determined to stop them. He raced up and down the court, fighting for rebounds and blocking Stanford's shots.

"Come on, you guys," he yelled to his teammates. "We can beat them!" Finally, UCLA gained the lead and went on to win the game. The fans went wild with joy.

When the season ended, UCLA had won more games than any other team in its conference. UCLA was named the champion. Each player on the team was given a little gold basketball to wear on a chain. During the next two years, Ralph collected two more. He treasured them more than anything he had ever owned.

Because of his love for athletics, Ralph was made sports editor of the college yearbook. He was still interested in making speeches and was president of his debating club. He also worked on the daily school paper and in the student government.

Although the school year was busy for Ralph, he didn't rest during vacations. For three summers he worked on a ship that traveled up and down the Pacific Coast. The money he made helped with his school expenses.

Early in his senior year, Ralph began to think about his future. As usual he talked things over with Nana.

"I need more education if I'm going to teach in a college," he said. "I'll need a master's degree."

"Well, nobody ever had too much education," Nana said, rocking in her favorite chair. "Could you get another scholarship?"

"They call it a fellowship when it's for

a graduate degree, Nana," Ralph said. "I think I'll apply for one at Harvard University."

"My grandson—at Harvard University. Think of that!" Nana said proudly.

"Hey, I haven't got the fellowship yet," Ralph said, laughing.

"But you will," Nana said firmly. "I know you will." And indeed he did.

Graduation day arrived, and the family gathered to watch Ralph receive his diploma—with highest honors. As they congratulated him, Ralph realized how much he would miss them all. Harvard was all the way across the country—in Cambridge, Massachusetts.

The day after graduation, Harvard began to seem even farther away. Ralph discovered that his fellowship did not cover travel and living expenses. How could he raise the necessary money? Perhaps he'd been foolish even to think about going to Harvard.

Help arrived unexpectedly. A black women's club in Los Angeles heard that Ralph needed money. The club raised a thousand dollars and presented it to him. Ralph was stunned. He'd never seen a check for so much money.

"How—how can I thank you?" he stammered to the club president.

"You've given the Los Angeles basketball fans a lot of pleasure," she said. "We're happy that you have a chance to go to Harvard. This check may show you how proud we are of you."

Speechless, Ralph shook her hand. "I'm really going to Harvard," he thought. "Nana was right. Nana's *always* right."

4. "How Can I Tell You?"

"Dear Nana," Ralph wrote, "Harvard is a great university, but I wish it were nearer to you." Ralph had received his master's degree in government in the spring of that year—1928. He had then decided to stay and study for a doctor's degree in political science. The money from another fellowship and a part-time job in a bookstore helped pay his way.

Nana wrote and told him how proud she was. She also sent many warnings to take good care of himself. One day in

November she wrote to ask if he would finish at Harvard that year. "She misses me," Ralph thought.

A few days later Aunt Nelle telephoned from Los Angeles. Ralph knew at once that something was wrong. "What is it? Is Nana all right?"

"How can I tell you?" Nelle said. "She died in her sleep last night."

There was silence on Ralph's end of the line.

"Are you still there, Ralph?" Nelle asked. "Ralph, I know how you feel. We'll all miss her terribly."

He choked out the words, "Get roses for her grave, Aunt Nelle. Good night, now." Slowly he put down the phone and dropped his head into his hands. Memories of Nana came rushing back. That tiny, lovely woman! He had hoped she'd live forever.

Soon after Nana's death, Ralph was offered a job as a teacher at Howard University, a fine all-black college in Washington, D.C. There was no political science department at Howard, and Ralph was asked to start one. This was an honor for a man so young. Ralph accepted the job. He was happy to be helping other blacks and to be doing something 'he really liked.

Soon Ralph had another reason to be happy. He met Ruth Harris, a pretty schoolteacher who was from Montgomery, Alabama. She was teaching elementary school and studying at Howard at night. Before long they were seeing each other every day.

In the spring of 1930 they were married. Ruth continued to teach until 1932 when their first daughter, Joan, was born.

Ralph's days were full and busy. He

took courses at Harvard toward his doctor's degree whenever he could spare the time. For relaxation, he played tennis or billiards or watched a baseball game. He had many good friends at Howard, and his students liked him. But he was not happy about the way blacks were treated in Washington, D.C. They were not allowed in most hotels, restaurants, and theaters. When Ralph rode on a bus, he had to stand in the crowded back end with the other black people.

Ralph hoped to go abroad to complete work on his degree. The doctoral program he was taking in government and international affairs required such study, but Ralph had another reason for wanting to go. He felt that the problems of black people everywhere were similar to those of blacks in the United States. He wanted to study black people in other countries at first hand. He particularly wanted to see how they were treated in Africa, where many of the black nations were colonies, governed by white nations.

Ralph discussed his feelings with Ruth. "If I could get another fellowship," he said, "I'd like to study some of the African colonies for my doctor's thesis. The trouble is, it would mean leaving you and Joan."

"Don't worry about us, Ralph," Ruth said. "We'll be fine. And I know how much the degree means to you."

Ralph got a fellowship that enabled him to make the trip. He visited two French-governed countries on the west coast of Africa—Togoland and Dahomey.

He met and talked with as many people as he could, asking questions and making notes. He saw how the Africans lived and how they were treated by the French, and

he learned how the governments operated. Then he returned home with his briefcase stuffed with notes.

Soon after his return, Ralph went to Harvard to write his thesis. It won a prize as the best in his field. Ralph became the first black man in America to earn a doctor's degree in political science.

Ralph returned to teaching at Howard. Later in that year of 1934, a second daughter, Jane, was born to the Bunches.

Ralph's trip to Africa had made him want to learn more about black people throughout the world. He asked for still another fellowship and got it. First, he studied anthropology and colonial government at colleges in the United States, England, and Africa. Then he studied people in their own countries.

Before Ralph went abroad, an African friend told him, "You must visit my tribe, the Kikuyu. They will treat you well." He promised to write and tell them Ralph was coming.

When he arrived in Africa, Ralph was amazed at the welcome the Kikuyu gave him. They made him feel as if he were one of them. Ralph told them of his great-great-grandfather, who had lived in

Africa long ago. Later Ralph wrote to
Ruth about his joyful "homecoming."

Ralph also visited Indonesia, Malaya,
Hawaii, and the Philippine Islands. He
studied the people and their cultures. The
results of his studies were published in
1937 in a booklet, *A World View of Race.*
Ralph wrote that race relations was a
worldwide problem. But, he said, there was
no reason for believing that people were
different because of the color of their skins.

Ralph returned to Washington, D.C., the
following year. Howard welcomed him back
by making him a full professor.

5. War Years

Ralph couldn't believe how his children had grown while he was gone. Joan was in school now—an all-black school miles away from their home. Although there was a school near the Bunche house, only white children were allowed there.

"It's so unfair," Ralph told Ruth. "Someday Washington will have to change. But I'm afraid it will be too late for our children."

Ralph attended regular meetings of the National Association for the Advancement of Colored People, the NAACP. He was glad black people were finally banding together to try to get rights equal to those of white people. The blacks wanted better education and better jobs. But Ralph could see that little progress was being made.

A chance came for Ralph to help in another way. Gunnar Myrdal, a Swedish expert in social studies, got in touch with Ralph. Myrdal planned to make a study of the American Negro. "You've studied living conditions of black people all over the world," he told Ralph. "Will you help me with my study?"

Ralph was excited. Never before had such a study been made. "It might lead the way to better understanding between blacks and whites," he told his wife.

Ralph, Gunnar Myrdal, and other experts traveled all over the country. They talked to blacks and whites in cities and towns, on farms and in factories.

One day they were questioning people in a small Southern town. Suddenly a tall, broad-shouldered sheriff appeared.

"Why are you asking all of those questions?" he growled. Ralph explained that they were making a study of the condition of blacks in America.

"Well, you'd better study someplace else," the sheriff warned. "Get out of

town before someone gets hurt." Ralph and Gunnar lost no time in getting back in their car.

Most white Southerners didn't want change in their way of life. They weren't going to allow blacks in their restaurants and hotels. And they weren't going to allow blacks to work at the better-paying jobs, which they considered white men's jobs.

The study took over two years. The hundreds of pages of notes that Ralph and Myrdal collected were expanded into a book called *An American Dilemma*. It was praised as "the best single factual report on the American Negro...."

Once again Ralph returned to teaching. He found that classes were getting smaller. It was 1941, and World War II was raging in Europe. Many young men were being called into the armed services as the United States prepared to defend itself.

"I wish I could join the army," Ralph told Ruth. "But I know I would be turned down because of my bad hearing." Ralph had trouble with the circulation in his legs too. They were often painful.

"There will be other ways you can help your country," Ruth said. "And I can't see you as a soldier. I don't think you could fight with anyone."

Ralph had to agree. He hated the thought of war. But if the United States were attacked, he would want to help.

The chance to serve his country soon came. The government was looking for someone with knowledge of Africa. If the war spread to the countries there, the United States would need to know as much as possible about them. Ralph was hired by the government as an expert on Africa and the Far East.

On December 7, 1941, the Japanese attacked the U. S. naval base at Pearl Harbor, Hawaii. Four days later Germany and Italy declared war on the United States.

Now that America was at war, Ralph's office was always crowded with people asking for information. North Africa had been occupied by Germany and Italy and was under their control. The American and British plan was to invade North Africa and then use it as a springboard to attack Italy.

Ralph's knowledge of the people and the region helped in planning the invasion of North Africa.

In November of 1942 nearly 300,000 American and British soldiers landed in North Africa. They forced the enemy to retreat and began to work their way through Italy and France toward Germany.

The war dragged on into 1944 with still no end in sight. Ralph was sad that bombing and suffering must go on. That year he was asked to join the State Department in a high-level job. He was the first black man to receive such an honor. But to Ralph and Ruth, something even more important happened. Another child was born.

"It's a fine, healthy boy," the doctor announced in the hospital waiting room.

Later Ruth said, "I guess we don't have to wonder what to call this one, do we? How does Ralph Johnson Bunche, Jr., sound?" Ralph smiled back—the smile of a proud father.

6. The United Nations Is Born

The San Francisco Opera House was half-filled when Ralph entered and found a seat. He looked up at the flags of many nations circling the back of the stage. He was thrilled by the thought of what those colorful flags meant.

It was April 25, 1945. Representatives from 50 countries were meeting in San Francisco to create the United Nations. Ralph was one of the United States' delegates to this meeting. The war was almost over, and the United States and its allies were sure of victory. Now they wanted to build a world organization that would insure a lasting peace.

"Millions of lives have been lost in this terrible war," Ralph thought. "The United Nations could mean a world free of war." He was proud to be a part of this meeting.

First, the representatives had to draw up a charter, which would describe the aims of the organization. Then rules had to be set up for its operation. The representatives were divided into groups to study and talk about each part of the charter.

Ralph was asked to work on the part of the charter concerning countries that were not self-governed. The UN hoped to help these countries learn to govern themselves. Some of them were countries that had come under foreign control because of earlier wars. Ralph had visited many of them.

His group spent long hours around a meeting table. Ralph worked at getting everyone's ideas down on paper.

Dr. Victor Hoo of China later told reporters, "He was the fastest draftsman I'd ever seen. He would listen to a discussion, no matter how complicated, and right away he would make a draft of it —adding his own ideas, which were always good."

When Ralph was not meeting with his own group, he attended meetings of all the representatives. It took two months for the representatives to agree on all parts of the charter.

The war in Europe had ended in May. Four months later Japan surrendered, and World War II was at last over. Ralph was glad that the soldiers could return home.

The newly formed United Nations began meeting in New York City. Ralph was asked to join the staff of the UN and took a leave of absence from the State Department in order to do so. In 1947 he gave up his job in the State Department, and the Bunches made plans to move to New York.

"You'll like it there, Ruth," Ralph said. "It's a better place for blacks than Washington. Little Ralph won't have to go to all-black schools as his sisters did." Ralph, Jr., was now three years old. The girls, thirteen and fifteen, were in a Quaker boarding school in Pennsylvania.

The Bunches found a comfortable place to live in Queens, an outlying part of New York City. Many other UN families lived there—people of all races and colors.

One of the first problems that faced the United Nations concerned Palestine. Long before the time of Christ, Palestine was the homeland of the Jews. Then the Romans conquered it, and many Jews were driven out. They settled in all parts of the world, for now they had no country of their own.

For centuries, Jewish people everywhere hoped and prayed for the return of their homeland. Then in the late 1800s and early 1900s, a movement called Zionism began to gather strength among European Jews. It called for the immigration of Jews to agricultural settlements in the Turkish colony of Palestine. By the end of World War I, there were 65,000 Jews living in Palestine, in the midst of a largely Arab population.

As a result of World War I, Turkey lost Palestine to the Allies. Great Britain was given the job of governing the area.

At first Great Britain promised the

Jews a homeland in Palestine. But then, as Arabs protested the increasing numbers of Jews settling in Palestine, the British began to limit Jewish immigration.

When Adolph Hitler and his Nazi Party rose to power in 1932, the Jews of Germany were deprived of all their rights and sent to concentration camps. When thousands of Jews fled Germany and sought refuge in Palestine, the Arabs reacted violently. In 1939, therefore, the British limited Jewish immigration to Palestine to 1,500 persons a month.

Then, during World War II, the Nazis began to send the Jews in the countries they occupied to death camps. Those who escaped the Nazi dragnet managed to make their way to Palestine, but the British held to their quota. Some refugees were smuggled into the country, but many others were turned back.

When the victorious Allies marched into Germany, they discovered that six million Jews had died in the Nazi death camps. Thousands of Jews had survived, but they were now homeless. The United States urged that 100,000 of them be allowed into Palestine. But there was more and more fighting now between Jews and Arabs. British forces were under attack too. Finally, Great Britain asked the United Nations to decide what should be done.

A special committee was appointed to study the problem. Ralph was one of those chosen. He made his first visit to Palestine.

Ralph spent much time at the many meetings with Arabs and Jews. In his free time he visited Jerusalem, a city holy to several religious faiths.

The committee decided that Britain

should no longer rule Palestine and that it should be divided, or partitioned, into three parts. The Arabs would have one part and the Jews another. The tiny third part, consisting only of Jerusalem, would be an international city. Its governor would be chosen by the United Nations.

The Arabs living in Palestine and in neighboring Arab states were angry. Why should the Jews be given land? Hadn't Arabs lived there for hundreds and hundreds of years?

"We'll drive the Jews out of Palestine!" they warned. Ralph hoped they would not carry out their threat. Surely Jews and Arabs could live peacefully side by side.

Ralph's committee reported to the UN General Assembly, which voted to divide Palestine.

The Jews of Palestine accepted the UN plan and began the task of organizing a government. The Arabs of Palestine were violently opposed to the plan and refused to set up their own government.

At midnight on May 14, 1948, a new Jewish nation was announced—the State of Israel. Within hours armies from neighboring Arab states attacked the newly formed country.

Ralph was saddened but not surprised at the news. "This will be the United Nations' first real test," he told a friend at work. "Can we keep the world at peace? It won't be easy. If we send in armies to stop the fighting, a small war might grow into a big one."

Ralph was asked to serve with a UN peacemaking group. It would be led by Count Folke Bernadotte of Sweden. The group would try to stop the fighting. Then it must persuade the Arabs to let the Jewish nation live in peace.

At the United Nations, Count Bernadotte (center) reports on the truce arranged between the two forces, Israeli (left) and Arab (below). Dr. Bunche is seated behind Count Bernadotte.

Count Folke Bernadotte was a tall, distinguished-looking man. Ralph found him to be warm and friendly. As their plane crossed the Atlantic, the two got to know each other. Ralph told Bernadotte what he had learned about Palestine.

Headquarters for the group were set up on the Greek island of Rhodes, not far from Palestine. During the next few weeks, Ralph and Bernadotte met first with Israeli, then with Arab leaders.

Progress was slow, for many people did not want peace. Terrorists even threatened to kill the count and Ralph.

At last both sides agreed to stop fighting. A four-week truce was declared.

"Congratulations!" Ralph said, shaking the count's hand. "You did it!" But each knew it was only a first step. The Arabs must agree to live peacefully beside the State of Israel.

7. The Struggle for Peace

One day in September Count Bernadotte said to Ralph, "We have a meeting in Jerusalem this afternoon. Shall we fly together?"

Ralph, his shirtsleeves rolled up, was working at his desk. "I still have to finish a report," he said. "I'll join you in Jerusalem as soon as I can."

All through the summer of 1948, the truce had been extended again and again. Meanwhile, both sides were gathering more guns and ammunition. Ralph wondered if the Arabs and Israelis would ever come to a permanent peace agreement.

He hurried with his work and then boarded a plane. When he landed, several UN aides were waiting for him.

"We have terrible news, Dr. Bunche," one of them said. "Count Bernadotte is dead."

Ralph was frozen with shock and sorrow. He finally managed to ask, "How did it happen?"

An hour earlier, he was told, Bernadotte and three other men had been in a UN car on their way to the meeting. They were stopped by a jeep filled with armed men. Three of the men jumped down from the jeep and fired into the car. Bernadotte was badly wounded and died shortly afterward in a hospital. A French colonel who had been sitting next to Count Bernadotte was killed instantly.

The colonel had taken Ralph's usual seat. Ralph realized that the bullet had probably been meant for him.

"The man I admired most in the world is dead," Ralph told a friend. "His only crime was in trying to bring peace to a troubled country."

Ralph was appointed acting mediator to take Bernadotte's place. His life was in great danger. Soon he began to receive threatening letters saying, "You'll get what Bernadotte got." Ralph worried far more about the huge task facing him than about the chance that he might be killed.

In the months that followed, Ralph worked at a back-breaking pace with little rest. The Arabs refused to admit that there was a State of Israel. The Israelis were determined not to leave the land they had been driven from almost 2,000 years before.

In December war broke out again. Now Israeli troops forced the armies of the Arab countries out of the new state.

Ralph was tired and discouraged. He decided that a few days with his family would help him, so he flew home for Christmas. He invited Countess Bernadotte to join his family for the holidays.

"It's an honor to have you in our home," Ralph said.

"It was kind of you to ask me," she said. "My husband told me what a great help you were to him." She looked sadly at his picture on the bookcase. It was signed "To Ralph with deepest gratitude for your devotion and loyalty—Folke Bernadotte."

"I feel richer for having known him," Ralph said.

Early on Christmas morning Ruth, the children, and Countess Bernadotte opened the presents Ralph had brought from Rhodes. In the cheerful living room stood a brightly lit Christmas tree. It was hard to believe that war was raging in the Middle East.

Ralph returned to Rhodes more rested than he had been in months. Again he began to plead with Arabs and Israelis to meet at Rhodes. At last they agreed to start talks. "This is a giant step forward," Ralph told an assistant.

At first the delegations from Israel and from the Arab countries met only with Ralph and his staff, not with each other. Ralph did not try to force them. He acted as a mediator, first meeting with one delegation, then another. He praised all the delegations for coming to Rhodes.

Finally, Ralph managed to bring the leaders of the Israeli and the Egyptian delegations into a meeting room together.

The Israeli held out his hand to the Egyptian. But the Arab walked past him and sat down. Ralph was stunned. He had worked so hard to arrange this meeting. Now the Israeli was deeply insulted.

Ralph hurried through the meeting, doing most of the talking himself. When it was over, he learned that the Israeli delegation was about to leave Rhodes in anger. Ralph took the Egyptian leader aside and asked him to smooth over the incident. Then he rushed to the Israelis and begged them not to go.

The second meeting got off to a better start. The Egyptian leader shook *both* hands of the Israeli. Soon the two were chattering together in Arabic. Suddenly they stopped, realizing that Ralph could not understand the language. Ralph, with a big grin on his face, motioned for them to go on. At last they were talking to

In Jerusalem UN observers inspect the new boundary which divides the war-torn city into two parts. Below, Ralph, at the microphone, presides at the signing of the final armistice agreement.

each other. Now they could get down to the business of settling their differences.

Ralph's first task was to make them agree to still another cease-fire. He held meetings all day long and often through the night. As always, he remained calm, friendly, and polite. His secretary said, "I never once saw him lose his temper. Whenever things got bad, he simply took a few minutes off and played billiards. Then he came back and got to work again."

"I'll stay here for ten years if I must," Ralph told reporters. "I'm not going to give up." At last, cease-fire agreements were signed.

Now boundaries had to be agreed on. Often days would be spent in deciding the ownership of one small town. Slowly progress was being made. Finally, delegations from four of the five Arab nations that had invaded Israel signed separate agreements with Israel to respect each other's boundaries. (Iraq, whose territory did not border on Israel, did not sign an agreement.)

Beaming, Ralph walked to a closet off the meeting room. He took out some beautiful pieces of pottery. He'd had them made weeks before and stored them in the closet.

Ralph gave these gifts to the Arabs and Israelis.

A surprised Israeli asked, "What would you have done with these if we had not agreed?"

"I'd have smashed them over your heads!" Ralph said with a laugh. Everyone in the room joined in the laughter.

Ralph cabled the good news to UN headquarters. Then he phoned Ruth. At last he could go home.

8. A Hero's Welcome

Ralph stood at the ship's rail as the *Queen Mary* steamed into New York Harbor. As always, he felt a thrill when the Statue of Liberty came into sight.

As the ship docked, his eyes searched the waiting crowd for Ruth's face. Then at last he saw her, holding five-year-old Ralph, Jr., high in her arms, so he could wave to his father. Ralph waved back and hurried to meet them.

He kissed Ruth and hugged little Ralph. Newspaper reporters crowded around the family.

"Do you think the war in Palestine is really over, Dr. Bunche?"

"Will you pose for a photograph with your family, Dr. Bunche?"

Flashbulbs flared and cameras snapped. Ralph could not believe it. When he'd first visited Palestine in 1947, hardly anyone had ever heard of him. Now he was being treated like a hero.

Later, crowds cheered as the Bunches were driven through the streets of New York in a parade. When at last they reached their home in Queens, Ralph said, "That was the hardest thing I've had to do yet. I don't know what all the fuss was about."

"You might as well get used to being famous," Ruth said. "Just look at this stack of mail waiting for you."

There was even more mail at his UN office. During the next few months, Ralph

received hundreds of letters asking him to speak. People wanted to learn more about the United Nations. And they wanted to meet the man who had stopped a war.

Ralph accepted 70 of the invitations. He felt it was important that he speak. He wanted to tell of his faith in the United Nations as a keeper of peace.

Ralph asked Ruth to go with him on his travels around the country. Together they visited city after city. Everywhere they were met by large crowds.

Los Angeles held a "Ralph Bunche Day" with a parade through the streets. Afterward Ralph was told that his name was being placed on the honor roll of his high school class of 1922. Ralph smiled with tight lips. He thought, "It only took 27 years to get it there. Now it doesn't matter that I'm black." But he said simply, "Thank you."

It was a long, exhausting tour, and the Bunches were glad when they could return home again. A short time later President Truman asked Ralph to be assistant secretary of state. Ralph thought the offer over, but he refused it. Newspaper reporters asked him why he had refused to accept the highest government position ever offered to a black person.

"I will tell you why," Ralph said. "Washington is no place for blacks. I have no desire to take my family back there."

There were still many places in the capital where black people were not allowed. The schools had not changed. In New York Ralph, Jr., would go to the UN's International School when he was old enough. There children from all over the world studied and played together.

His daughters were at college now—one at Vassar and one at Radcliffe.

Ralph returned to his work at the UN, happy to be back among friends of all races. Life had been good to him, he thought.

Ralph's happiness was destroyed when, during the summer of 1950, six-year-old Ralph, Jr., became ill. He had a high fever, a headache, and a sore throat.

"It's polio," the doctor said after the boy had been taken to the hospital for tests.

Polio! A dreaded disease that could kill or leave one crippled or unable to move at all! At that time there was no vaccine that could prevent the disease. Ralph put his arm around Ruth as fear for their son struck them.

"He'll have the best of care," the doctor promised. "But you won't be able to see him for a while. It's possible you could get polio too. But try not to worry." He patted Ruth's shoulder.

The days dragged by as Ruth and Ralph prayed for the boy to get well. At last they were allowed to see him.

"You're going to be all right, son," Ralph said, hoping he sounded sure. Every day he and Ruth spent hours at the boy's bedside. They read to Ralph, Jr., and helped keep up his spirits. Slowly the boy began to get better. He was pale and thin but unharmed by the disease.

Ruth baked a cake to celebrate her son's homecoming. Ralph thought that the day was better than any birthday. He'd been given a present of his son's life.

Soon afterward Ralph received another present. A cable arrived, telling him that he had been awarded the Nobel Peace Prize. It was for his part in bringing an

Ralph Bunche accepts the Nobel Peace Prize for his work in bringing about an end to the Arab-Israeli war of 1948. At right, he accepts the congratulations of his children, Joan and Ralph, Jr.

end to the Arab-Israeli war. This prize is one of the highest honors in the world. Never before had it been given to a black man.

Newspapers everywhere headlined the news: GRANDSON OF A SLAVE WINS NOBEL PRIZE. Memories of that slave, Nana, came pouring back to Ralph. How proud she would have been!

9. Keeping the Peace

"There's trouble in Egypt," Ralph's secretary said, handing him a report. Ralph sighed and took the report to study it. It was July of 1956. He had been given the high post of undersecretary of the United Nations the year before. Ralph worked on solving many different problems. But Middle Eastern problems were still his specialty.

Egypt had seized the Suez Canal. Although the canal runs through Egypt, it was owned by a world group. All nations had been able to use this important canal, which connects the Mediterranean and Red seas, but now the Egyptians alone would control it.

In spite of the armistice agreements, there was still scattered fighting between Israel and Egypt. Therefore, Egypt said that Israeli ships would not be allowed in the canal.

Ralph put down the report and paced the floor. "After all the work of the UN," he thought, "this will mean war again."

Britain and France had been the most important members of the group that had operated the canal. Now they joined the Israelis in invading Egypt. President Eisenhower asked the warring countries to let the United Nations settle the matter.

The UN put together an army of men from different countries to try to keep peace. It was called the United Nations

Emergency Force (UNEF). Ralph was to be in charge of the 6,000-man force. By November UNEF was organized, and soldiers were sent to Egypt. They were ordered not to fight but to prevent fighting.

For the next four years, Ralph spent most of the time traveling. He directed the peace-keeping efforts in the Middle East. He also advised the African nations that were working toward independence from their European rulers. He enjoyed helping these blacks become independent.

But Ralph was weary from all his years of hard work, and his health was poor. His legs were painful. His eyesight was failing. And he was suffering from a disease called diabetes.

"It would be nice," he told Ruth, "to stop working and enjoy my family." Jane was already married and had two children.

As director of the UN Emergency Force, Ralph made field trips to inspect its work at first hand. He is seen at Gaza talking to Arab children (above) and in the headquarters of the Yugoslav Battalion (below).

Ralph felt that he never had enough time to spend with his growing family. Still, the work of the United Nations was too important to give up.

When he managed to get home, Ralph spent as much time as possible with his son. Ralph, Jr., was fifteen in the summer of 1959. He began taking tennis lessons at a nearby club.

"Dad," he said one day, "my tennis coach suggested I become a junior member of the club. Then I could play there all the time, instead of only on my lesson day. Could I?"

Ralph looked up from the baseball game they had been watching on television. "I'll check into it, son," he promised. He'd heard that this club would not allow blacks as members.

The club president told Ralph flatly that blacks were not accepted. "It's the same old story," Ralph thought. He felt deeply hurt for his son as well as for black people everywhere. He decided to let the newspapers hear of it. Headlines read: NOBEL PEACE PRIZE WINNER'S SON DENIED MEMBERSHIP IN CLUB.

People all over the country spoke out in anger. The club received hundreds of bitter letters. Later Ralph, Sr., was offered a membership in the club, but he refused to accept it.

The following year there was another crisis to handle in Africa. Belgium had ruled the Congo there since the early 1900s. Now the Congolese wanted to govern themselves. Belgium agreed to give them their independence on June 30, 1960.

Only a few days later, fighting broke out. Few Congolese had been educated or trained to run their country, so many

Belgians had remained in key jobs. Now the Congolese soldiers rebelled against their Belgian officers. Soon the lives of all whites were in danger, and they hurriedly left the country. When they had gone, Belgian planes and ships attacked the Congo.

The only hope of stopping the fighting lay in the United Nations. Once again Ralph was sent to direct peace-keeping forces. By now the Congolese leaders were fighting among themselves for control of the new nation. There was bitter civil war. Ralph knew that it might take many months or even years before problems in the Congo could be solved, but he was determined to restore peace.

As he traveled back and forth to Africa, Ralph sometimes thought of Miss Emma Belle Sweet's geography lessons. What a teacher she had been!

He was given a chance to show Miss Sweet how he felt about her in 1962. The National Education Association named Ralph the winner of their Gold Key award. It was for outstanding contributions to American life. Ralph was asked to name his favorite teacher.

"That would be Miss Emma Belle Sweet," Ralph answered without a moment's pause. "She would be pretty old by now. I hope she's still alive and well."

After a separation of 47 years, a beloved teacher and her famous pupil meet again.

Miss Sweet, 82 years old, was indeed alive and well. She was proud and happy to come East to be given a Gold Key also.

Ralph was glad to see her again. He showed her around the United Nations building. Reporters snapped pictures of them. Ralph was asked why he had chosen her as his favorite teacher.

"She was a very fine teacher," Ralph said. "But perhaps more important, she was a wonderful person. For the first time, I found someone who treated me just like everybody else."

Miss Sweet said, "There are many fine teachers who deserved this award more than I did. Not every sixth-grade teacher was so fortunate as to have a Ralph Bunche as one of her pupils."

But Ralph was still sure that *he* was the lucky one.

10. No End of Problems

"Isn't it time you slowed down, Ralph?" Ruth asked him on one of his rare visits home. "You work too hard."

"I can't slow down," Ralph said. "There's too much to be done." The thought of a world entirely at peace was his special dream. As long as there was something he could do to help make this dream come true, he would go on working.

The war in the Congo dragged on, and Ralph doubled his efforts to bring peace. More and more UN soldiers were brought

In his lifelong role as statesman and diplomat, Ralph Bunche...

- Met the press.
- Presented the position of the UN to world leaders.
- Listened carefully to the arguments of all groups.
- Traveled the world over to keep the peace.

in. By 1963 Ralph was in charge of 20,000 soldiers in the Congo, as well as a staff of hundreds.

At the same time, Ralph was directing the peace-keeping army in the Suez Canal area. There seemed to be no end of problems in the Middle East.

The pace at which Ralph worked was ruining his health. Early in 1971 he was ordered into the hospital. He tried to carry out his duties by phone from his bed in New York Hospital. At times he was well enough to go home. But he was in the hospital more often than not during the following months.

By June Ralph had to admit that he was too ill to continue his work. The secretary-general of the United Nations, U Thant, visited Ralph in the hospital.

"I must resign from the UN," Ralph said. "I can't be of use to you anymore."

"You've already been of more use than any other single person," Thant said. "Just think about getting well now."

Secretary-General Thant didn't announce Ralph's resignation to the newspapers until October. For months he had hoped and prayed that his good friend would regain his health and return to the UN. But it was not to be.

On December 9, 1971, Ralph Johnson Bunche died. He had given more than 25 years of his life to the United Nations. People the world over were saddened by his death.

At the United Nations building flags flew at half-mast. In the UN's General Session, U Thant read the first of many tributes praising Ralph. He said, "He was an outstanding example of that new twentieth-century breed of international officials, who devote all of their gifts and their very lives to the service of the community of mankind."

At Ralph Bunche's funeral these words were said: "He belonged to every nation on earth that yearns for peace.... Thank you, Ralph, and good-bye."

Index